Know About
Rani Lakshmibai

MAPLE KIDS

KNOW ABOUT RANI LAKSHMIBAI

ALL RIGHTS RESERVED. No part of this book may be reproduced in a retrieval system or transmitted in any form or by any means electronics, mechanical, photocopying, recording and or without permission of the publisher.

Published by

MAPLE PRESS PRIVATE LIMITED
office: A-63, Sector 58, Noida 201301, U.P., India
phone: +91 120 455 3581, 455 3583
email: info@maplepress.co.in
website: www.maplepress.co.in

Reprinted in 2019

ISBN: 978-93-50334-11-9

Contents

Preface 4
1. Rani's Early Years 5
2. Brave Young Girl 8
3. Arrival of the British 11
4. Manu's Marriage 14
5. Crushing Blow 18
6. Legal Complications 21
7. Withered Hope 25
8. Petitions to the British 28
9. Preparation for an Explosion 31
10. Insult upon Insult 34
11. Fuel in Fire 37
12. The Spreading Fire 40
13. Revolt in Jhansi 43
14. Rani's Control 46
15. Encounter with Sathe Khan 50
16. The Return of the British 54
17. Rani's Defence 57
18. The Siege of Jhansi 60
19. The Battle Continued 63
20. Jhalkari Korin 66
21. The Real Jhansi Massacre 70
22. The Final Battle 73
23. Account of Rani's Death 76
24. A Glorious Woman 79

Preface

Rani Lakshmibai, an epitome of bravery and courage, is a model for all Indian women. She influences and molds a definitive stereotype of strong will and determination. In earlier times, when the status of women in India was not that progressive, Rani Lakshmibai set an example of woman empowerment and their terms of equality to men.

The way she encouraged and inspired her people to fight against the British was remarkable. She emanated bravery and shook the roots of the British from the Indian land. Even the British officials were aware of her valour and heroism.

She is reverently remembered for her glory and bravery. Her determined soul and dedication for the country imprints her name in gold among other freedom fighters of India. This book takes an attempt to throw light on her illuminated life embellished in heroism, audacity and fearlessness making her an unforgettable legend.

Chapter 1
Rani's Early Years

Manikarnika, who came to be known as Rani Lakshmibai, was born on 19 November 1828 in Varanasi, Banaras. She was born to Bhagirathi Sapre and Moro Pant Tambe. Moro Pant Tambe was the chief political advisor to Baji Rao II, the brother of the last Peshwa of Bithori. Manikarnika grew up in the palace. Baji Rao II was a Peshwa only in name. In reality, his decisions were directed by the British East India Company. In return for his services, he was paid a pension of rupees eight lakh per year and was presented the '*jagir*' of Bithori.

Manikarnika was a reflection of her mother, Bhagirathi Sapre, who was a good-looking, cultured, intelligent and religious lady. Manikarnika featured a broad forehead, her eyes glowed like twin suns, and the radiance of her face reflected royalty. She lost her mother at a young age of four. The whole responsibility of bringing up the daughter fell on the father.

Baji Rao asked Moro Pant Tambe to return to Bithori. Manu became the darling child of Moro Pant. He took

utmost care of his daughter. Manikarnika was lovingly called '*Chabili*' by Baji Rao.

Her Childhood

Few years passed. As Baji Rao had no children, he adopted a boy and named him Dhondu Pant. He also became the guardian of his younger brothers, Bala Rao and Rao Saheb. Manu grew up with them. She received her education, and training in martial arts along with the boys. Manu had a keen interest in fencing, wrestling, shooting, and horse riding. Out of which, horse riding was her favourite sport.

She was quick-witted and determined. As precocious as she was, she became proficient in martial arts. She was particularly fascinated by military formations, breaking these formations and army manoeuvres. She greatly enjoyed clearing trenches on horseback and engaged in swordfight with a sword in each hand. She gave tough challenges to her companions and outshined them in such exercises. As time passed, she overcame her delicacy and went on to become a formidable warrior. She was strikingly beautiful and brave. She was proficient in both Hindi and Sanskrit.

Chapter 2
Brave Young Girl

Manu was heroic and adventurous. She read and drew inspiration from the tales of mighty and patriotic heroes like Shivaji and Maharana Pratap, and mythological heroes like Arjuna and Bhima.

By the age of twelve, Manu was a beautiful and brave girl. Moro Pant got worried about her marriage, as in those days, girls were married at a very young age. This custom was strictly followed, especially in the case of Brahmin girls, who were likely to be banished if they were not married before they completed twelve.

One evening, Manu with her brothers, went for riding across the plains of the Ganga near Bithori in Maharashtra. One of the boys challenged, "Watch how I'll ride my horse and beat you both hollow." He prompted the horse and the horse galloped like a bullet. The other boy, Nana, wanted to overtake him and pulled his horse's reins. The horse tried to catch up, but stumbled on a big stone and the boy fell on the ground. The horse ran away. The boy got injured and blood started oozing. The boy sat up, but was too scared to look at the blood. He called out Manu who was galloping away, "Manu, Manu... stop... Don't leave me here. I'm dying, look at the blood!" Manu, who was ahead of him, turned her horse and galloped back. She dismounted the horse and examined the wound. She assured him not to be afraid and ensured to take him back home to dress the wound so that it would heal soon.

With the hem of her skirt, she gently wiped the blood from the wound. By then the boy who had galloped away, came back and asked Nana, "What happened, Dhondu? Were you badly hurt?" The injured boy was Nana Dhondu and the other boy was Tantia Tope.

Manu reassured, "It's nothing serious. We can dress it as soon as we go back to the fort, it'll heal soon."

Manu placed Nana on the horse and sat behind him. She held the reins in one hand went back to the fort with Tantia following her. Even at a tender age, such was her bravery and valour!

Chapter 3
Arrival of the British

In the beginning of the nineteenth century, the British came to India for trade. Gradually they began to acquire political power in the name of the East India Company.

The British took the advantage of the conflicts between Indian Rajas and Maharajas, and made them their puppets. The British used every misfortune of India to expand their empire. The arrogance of the British knew no bounds when they removed the last Peshwa from power. They even brushed aside the Mughal Emperor.

On one hand, there was a constant effort to destroy freedom and on the other hand, attempts were made to get rid of slavery.

The love of freedom can never be suppressed. The more it is repressed, the stronger it grows. The native kings felt powerless and had to accept the humiliating conditions imposed by the East India Company government. The government marked their states as 'protected states'. People were growing furious to remove the British rule

and defend the country's freedom and honour. The country was transforming into a silent volcano, which seemed calm before a violent eruption.

Amidst these, there was an ongoing search to find a girl for the marriage of Raja of Jhansi, Gangadhar Rao.

One day, Dikshita Shastry, a brahmin scholar from Jhansi, came to meet Baji Rao. He was proficient in astrology. He studied the horoscope of Manu Bai and made his calculations. Suddenly, his eyes sparkled and he exclaimed, "Excellent! This is no ordinary horoscope Peshwaji. This girl may be destined to become a queen. May I see the girl?"

Baji Rao sent for Manu Bai. She entered like a gentle lightning, and hypnotized everyone with her smile. Shastry was astonished to see such a beautiful girl. Manu respectfully touched his feet. When he talked to Manu, he found her to be very intelligent.

Chapter 4
Manu's Marriage

Dikshita Shastry spoke to Moro Pant in confidence and told him the purpose of his visit. He requested Manu's hand in marriage for Gangadhar Rao.

At that time, Jhansi was the headquarters of a district in Uttar Pradesh. The treaty between the British and the Raja of Jhansi enclosed two conditions. Firstly, Jhansi should help the British, whenever they needed help and secondly, the consent of the British was necessary to decide who should be the ruler of Jhansi.

In 1838, Gangadhar Rao was appointed as the Raja by the British. The former Raja, Raghunath Rao had exploited the treasury. The administration had collapsed and the people of Jhansi had no peace. But under the peaceful rule of Gangadhar Rao, everything fell back to normal.

The palace acquired more cattle, elephants and horses. The armoury was well stocked with arms and ammunitions. The army had five thousand infantry and five hundred cavalry with some armaments.

❖ *Know About Rani Lakshmibai* ❖

Gangadhar Rao appointed witty, courageous and sophisticated men in high positions. The fort was guarded by competent generals. He paid special attention to remove any weaknesses of the forces and improvised his army. He was very humble and treated all men and women with equal consideration. He was liked and respected by his subjects.

But, the major problem was the huge treasury expense on the British army that was stationed in the state of Jhansi. Gangadhar Rao was a widower and had no children. He wished to marry again, and delegated the task of finding the eligible bride to Dikshita. Moro Pant agreed to give Manu Bai's hand in marriage to Gangadhar Rao. Dikshita spoke to Gangadhar Rao about Manu Bai after he returned to Jhansi and the marriage was settled.

On the auspicious day, the whole of Jhansi was gaily decorated. Their marriage was grandly celebrated, making Manu Bai the wife of Gangadhar Rao.

At that time, Manu Bai was thirteen and Gangadhar Rao was forty-seven. He lovingly called his wife 'Lakshmibai'. He promoted his father-in-law, Moro Pant, to a high position in Jhansi. So, Moro Pant got settled in Jhansi.

Jhansi was situated between the River Yamuna and the Vindhya Mountains. Previously, it was known as Bundel Khand. Jhansi was the capital of all the small states in the Bundel Khand region. Jhansi entailed a glorious history and was presumed to be stronger as compared to other states. All of its rulers were known for their courage and good governance.

After she became the queen, Lakshmibai stayed within the palace in the fort, but continued to practise horse riding, fencing and shooting. She also trained other women in the palace in these arts.

Gangadhar Rao and Lakshmibai led a happy life for some time. Rao was a just ruler. He undertook various welfare programmes for his people. He improved his military regime by acquiring more elephants and horses. The people of Jhansi were happy and prosperous under his rule.

At the age of sixteen, Lakshmibai gave birth to a son in 1851. Gangadhar was overjoyed and the occasion was cheerfully celebrated by the people of Jhansi.

Chapter 5
Crushing Blow

But unfortunately, the newborn died at the age of three months. This was an unbearable shock to Lakshmibai and Gangadhar Rao. He was mentally disturbed and became bed-ridden. He was worried about the future of the state. Lakshmibai was crushed by the death of her son and the following sickness of her husband. She spent all her days and nights in praying and taking care of her husband.

Gangadhar Rao's condition grew worse. The reason for his distress was his apprehension of the cruel rule to be followed by Lord Dalhousie, the Governor-General at that time. The British had helped some native rulers and in return, had imposed a condition that, if the ruler died without children, the British would take over the state. Even if the ruler adopted a son, the adopted son would not have any ruling powers. Lord Dalhousie formulated a policy that a yearly pension would be fixed for the descendants and that the British Government would take the full responsibility for protecting the state.

The British controlled many native states through this policy. Now they had their eyes on Jhansi. This was a serious blow for Maharaja Gangadhar Rao, who was already old. Since he had no children, he decided to adopt Anand Rao, the son of a distant relative. The Maharaja and Lakshmibai adopted Anand Rao as their son in 1853, during the *'Dusshera'* festival. He was named Damodar Rao. Merriment and celebration filled the state once again!

To ensure that the British understood the adoption was proper and legal, the local British officials, the political agent, Major Ellis, and Captain Martin, were called to witness the event. He prepared a will, requesting the British to treat Damodar as his true son, and that Lakshmibai should rule Jhansi, after Gangadhar's death. The will was read to Major Ellis, and repeated in a letter to the political agent of Gwalior and Bundelkhand, Major Malcolm.

Gangadhar's grandfather had signed a treaty with the British, which tied him and his heirs and successors to Jhansi in perpetuity. The history of the succession had been complicated due to previous childless successions, British interventions in the state's administration, and additional treaties. Nevertheless, the rulers of Jhansi had been pro-British since the time of the initial treaty and nobody anticipated that there would be a problem with the succession.

Doctrine of Lapse: This policy was established by Lord Dalhousie during British rule. According to this policy, an Indian king could not transfer his kingdom to his adopted children in the absence of natural heirs. Thus, his kingdom came naturally under British rule.

Chapter 6
Legal Complications

After the celebrations of the adoption were over, Gangadhar Rao wrote a letter to the Company. He gave all the details about the adoption and requested the Company to recognise the adopted son as the legal heir. He suggested that, till Damodar Rao attained the age to rule, Rani Lakshmibai should be recognised as his rightful representative. The Maharaja re-emphasized the friendly relations that Jhansi shared with the East India Company. The letter was handed over by the Maharaja to Major Ellis requesting him to give it to Lord Dalhousie.

The Maharaja was sorrowful, while handing over the letter. It was a moment of great emotional turmoil, even, the Maharani was crying behind the curtain.

Gangadhar Rao said to the Major, "Major Saheb, my Rani is a woman. But she characterizes many qualities which would draw appreciation from the ablest of men." Gangadhar Rao's eyes filled with tears as he was speaking.

"Major Saheb, please see that on no account Jhansi becomes an orphan" he said.

On 21 November 1853, Gangadhar Rao died. The inexperienced 18-years-old Lakshmibai became a widow. Suddenly she was wrapped in the cruel chains of custom and Hinduism. But Gangadhar Rao had willed that Lakshmibai would not become a '*sati*'. Additionally, the Rani declined that 'honour'. The British had outlawed the practice of '*sati*' in 1829. In fact, Lakshmibai limited her official mourning activities to the minimum. She stayed inside for the minimum period of 13 days. She did not portray herself as a widow and did not shave her head, break her bangles or dress in white.

In the meantime, Baji Rao had also died. The East India Company stopped the payment of the annual pension of eight lakh rupees, even though the Company had solemnly affirmed that the pension would continue as per the agreement. Young Dhondu Pant became very furious at the treachery of the Company and decided to revolt against the British.

The British captured states on some pretext or the other. They took over Lucknow and Avadh, and dislodged the Emperor in Delhi. Several big states were now under their control. The cowardice of the Nawabs and Rajas made things easier for the British. The British not only expanded their territories, but also preached their religion in dubious ways. They employed all possible methods to weaken powerful states and increase their own power. This irked the country men to fight for their freedom and men like Nana and Tantia Tope were planning to revolt against the British.

The responsibility to defend the unprotected state of Jhansi fell on the young shoulders of Lakshmibai. The plight of Lakshmibai was unexplainable. On one side was Dalhousie, who was waiting to capture the kingdom and on the other side was Damodar Rao, an infant in her arms.

Chapter 7

Withered Hope

Lakshmibai sent a number of petitions to Dalhousie for a decision on Maharaja's will. Three months passed, but she failed to get any reply.

On one unfortunate day, in March 1854, Dalhousie's order finally arrived. It read that the Company has failed to recognise the right of late Maharaja Gangadhar Rao's adoption of an heir. Therefore they have decided to merge Jhansi in the British provinces. The letter further ordered Rani to vacate the fort and shift to a palace in the city. She will be paid a monthly pension of rupees five thousand." The Rani could not believe it at first. She was shocked at the decision for some time, and then exclaimed, "No, impossible, I shall not surrender my Jhansi."

The people of Jhansi were dismayed. The generals of the army were infuriated and suggested that Jhansi should declare war against the British. But, Rani held her patience and restrained from revolting. She strategically planned to equip and prepare Jhansi before declaring for war. It did not take her long to realise how difficult it was for the

small state of Jhansi to fight against the British. The kings of Delhi and even the Peshwas had surrendered before it.

In no time, Major Ellis brought Jhansi under the Company's control. He took the possession of the keys of the offices and announced the takeover of the administration by the Company.

After the British took over the government, Rani Lakshmibai was moved to a palace outside the court. She was granted a monthly pension of rupees five thousand, a palace, state jewels and funds. But, she was required to pay the Raja's debts, which should have been paid out of state funds.

As a high caste Hindu woman, Rani was expected to observe *'purdah'*, but with the death of her husband, she cast that aside. She was one of the richest people, if not the richest person, in Jhansi. And being the queen, she conducted business both with the British and with local personages. All her subjects revered and called upon her to exercise the duties of the office.

Chapter 8
Petitions to the British

Rani followed a strict routine. Every morning, the wee hours from four to eight were set apart for bathing, worship, meditation and prayer. From eight to eleven, she would go for horse riding, practice shooting, swordsmanship and shooting with arrows, with the reins held with the teeth. Thereafter, she would bathe again, give food, shelter and clothing to the poor and then have food, after which she

rested for a while. She used to undertake light exercises in the evening. Later in the evening, she used to go through some religious books and hear religious sermons, worship her deity. It was then followed by supper. All things were done systematically, strictly following the timetable.

The reason behind the capture of Jhansi was not because it was ruled by a Rani as it was not unusual for a woman to rule a state in India, or England for that matter. Nor was it due to any doubts as to her ability to govern. The British political agent, Major Malcolm, wrote that, "The Rani was highly respected and esteemed, and I believe she is fully capable of doing justice to such a charge." He was not alone in that opinion and, as later events have undoubtedly proved it, it was wholly justified. The annexation was due to the excessive greed of the British for power.

On 3 December 1853, Rani appealed against the decision. The local political agent, Major Ellis, wrote a letter in support of her case. Perhaps, Malcolm got a hint of the political wind and did not forward it. On 16 February 1854, she appealed for the second time. Both the appeals were refused. It was after her decision on 15 March 1854 that the Rani famously supposed to have exclaimed '*Jhansi nahin dungi*' (I will not give up my Jhansi.) Then she locked herself away for three days, refusing to eat or drink.

Then, she thought it would be better to appoint a British counsel and employed John Lang. He was in India and had opinioned against the Company in the courts. She drafted her third appeal on 22 April 1854, with Lang's assistance. It followed an appeal to the Court of Directors in London, but in vain.

Her repeated petitions till 1856 seemed to have irritated Dalhousie. Those, who had examined the case, agreed that the capture was not justified and that it was against the treaty of 1817, and therefore, Dalhousie's case was incorrect. The East India Company did not have to answer to any proper court of law. With the Policy of Lapse and its implementation, it unconsciously overstepped the mark and contributed to the 1857 Rebellion.

Chapter 9
Preparation for an Explosion

People became victims to injustice and tyranny. The Company tightened the security arrangements, which questioned the freedom of the people. An order was issued for the people to submissively salute the British officers who commuted in palanquins. The people were enraged. They were ready to revolt against the British but once again the Rani held them back. "Let us not be hasty. I am the queen of a state and yet I have been accepting a pension of five thousand rupees, do you know why? Some day our state will be ours, once again. Until then let us not betray our true feelings. Let us grow stronger and then challenge them; until then, patience should be our watchword."

Everybody was dismayed including the king who lost their kingdoms because they had no sons, the members of their families, their dependents, the disbanded army and the well-wishers of all these people.

Lovers of freedom, like Tantia Tope, Raghunath Simha and Jawahar Simha secretly went to meet Rani Lakshmibai.

They used to give her details regarding the dissatisfaction and discontent of the people.

Rani Lakshmibai carefully studied the geography of her kingdom. She focussed on the strategic points and the formation of the Sikh army of Punjab in its fight against the British.

Her determination sharpened with each passing day. She used to meet Tantia Tope and shared her plans with him. Some of her relatives, who were Rajputs also met her. While, pouring the holy water of Ganga on their swords, they swore that they would fight for 'her'. Rani became more hopeful and determined. She gathered the women of the palace and began to train them in fighting.

Whenever she went out, she used to put on warriors' accoutrement, a metallic helmet, a metallic coat, pyjamas and a tight waistband. She used to carry a pistol on both sides, and two swords in two sheaths. When she rode on horse, she used to tightly hold the reins between the teeth and wield swords and spears as the horse thundered along. Lakshmibai was well acquainted with the characteristic marks and the mettle of different types of horses. '*Kathiyawar*', the horse that is spotless white in colour, was her favourite horse.

As Rani Lakshmibai had flowing hair, it was difficult for her to wear the helmet and tie the turban over it. In Maharashtra, widows were supposed to shave their heads. Rani decided to get her hair shaved at Banaras. Her main aim was to study the political situation in that part of the country. She had to take the permission of the British officials, but they did not permit her journey.

Rani felt insulted and took an oath, "I will cut my hair only after the country gains freedom or otherwise it can take place only in the cemetery."

Chapter 10
Insult upon Insult

Time passed and the adopted son, Damodar Rao, completed six years and entered the seventh. Rani wanted to celebrate his '*Upanayana*', a religious celebration to ritualize him with the sacred thread.

It was a religious celebration, but there was another reason behind it. The harassment and torture of the people by the British was worrying Rani and she had to take some

important decisions. So, she had to consult other leaders who had grievances against the British. The 'upanayana' appeared to be a good opportunity for this. It would become the juncture where all the leaders could meet.

The dissatisfied Nana Saheb and Rao Saheb, Bahadur Shah, the King of Delhi, and the well-wishers of the Nawab of Avadh, were all anxious to meet.

Rani sent a petition to the British officer-in-charge of the state. There were six lakh rupees in the treasury in Damodar Rao's name. Rani asked for the permission to withdraw a lakh of rupees for the religious ceremony.

But she felt terribly insulted, when she received the Company's reply which stated, "The amount can be advanced only if four wealthy citizens stand as guarantors. When Damodar Rao comes of age, either the citizens or the queen shall pay him the required amount. But the amount the Rani asks for can be paid only if four wealthy citizens stand security."

The Rani swallowed the insult and hid her fury. Sixty-two leading citizens of Jhansi willingly offered to give her the money, but she was allowed to spend the money, which belonged to her. At last, the Company paid the amount on the word of four leading citizens.

The 'upanayana' was a lavish and grand affair. The leaders met for the religious ceremony.

Some women were appointed to keep a strict watch all around the place, as the leaders held their meeting.

The leaders had some information. The Hindu soldiers in the British army were infuriated because they were not allowed to wear the '*tilak*' on their foreheads and the bullets were tarnished with animal fat. The soldiers had to bite the bullet in order to remove the cover and use it. Both the Hindu and Muslim soldiers were enraged. There was deep discontent in the army, but she was still not ready to revolt. Rani ensured that the war be devoid of any looting or *dacoity*. Everyone agreed with Rani.

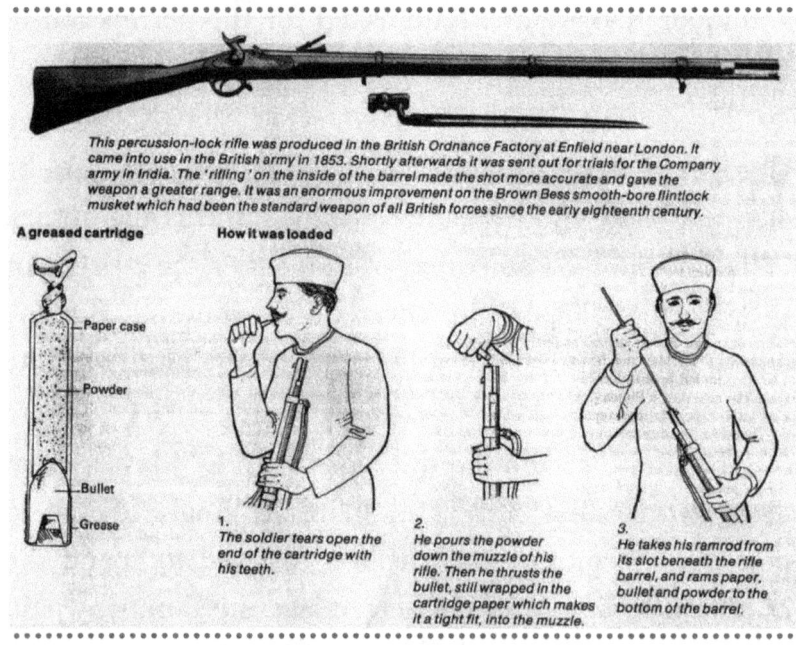

This percussion-lock rifle was produced in the British Ordnance Factory at Enfield near London. It came into use in the British army in 1853. Shortly afterwards it was sent out for trials for the Company army in India. The 'rifling' on the inside of the barrel made the shot more accurate and gave the weapon a greater range. It was an enormous improvement on the Brown Bess smooth-bore flintlock musket which had been the standard weapon of all British forces since the early eighteenth century.

A greased cartridge
- Paper case
- Powder
- Bullet
- Grease

How it was loaded

1. The soldier tears open the end of the cartridge with his teeth.
2. He pours the powder down the muzzle of his rifle. Then he thrusts the bullet, still wrapped in the cartridge paper which makes it a tight fit, into the muzzle.
3. He takes his ramrod from its slot beneath the rifle barrel, and rams paper, bullet and powder to the bottom of the barrel.

Chapter 11
Fuel in Fire

India is a vast country of people, cultures, fertile soils and lands. The British found a ready market for their trade. They could freely buy raw materials at cheaper rates, sell their finished products four times its actual price to the same people, and fill their treasury. The lack of unity among Indians fuelled the success of the East India Company.

Even though they controlled India's political and economic sphere, they influenced the religious sphere as well. They promoted Christianity amongst the Indians. Thus, there were several reasons behind people's agitation.

By 1857, the rage against the British began to manifest as a revolt. The mutiny was limited to the north of India, mainly the Gangetic Plains.

The women also engaged in fanning dissatisfaction among the army camps through various methods like songs in fairs, etc. The Rani was kept informed about each and every happening.

In a pitch-dark night in February, Tantia Tope came to meet the Rani. Tantia brought with him a handbill that

read, "It is impossible to suffer any more. How long can we bear the agony of the dagger pierced through the heart? Awaken and sacrifice for the love for your country. Some tyrants have kept this country in subjection. Drive them away. Free the country, uphold the right."

Rani felt that it was still not the right time. Tantia said that there was extreme dissatisfaction in the army. Also, the required money could be arranged and the arms and ammunitions were ready. It was decided that the revolt would rise on 31 May 1857.

The rebels chose lotus and '*roti*' as their symbols. The lotus is the emblem of greatness of Saraswati, the Goddess of knowledge, and Lakshmi, the Goddess of wealth. The '*roti*' sustains life. The villages who wanted to participate in the revolt would send a fresh '*roti*' to the neighbouring village and so the message would spread.

But before the date, the trouble broke out in Barrackpur. On May 10, the spark of revolt blazed up in Meerut. The Indian army of Meerut and Delhi merged and established their authority over the throne of Delhi. The dethroned Mughal ruler Bahadur Shah Zafar was proclaimed as the Emperor of India.

Bahadur Shah Zafar's Flag-1857

This flag was used by Bahadur Shah Zafar during the First War of Independence in 1857. It had a lotus and a chapati on

Chapter 12
The Spreading Fire

There was no change in her daily routine as she prepared for the war along with her usual religious discourses. Once she was questioned by her bosom friend asking the necessity for preparing herself for the war and prioritizing it over religion. To which she answered, "I am a *'Kshatriya'* woman, and I am doing my duty. It is the duty of a *Kshatriya* to protect the country and justice. If necessary, we must be prepared to fight. I cannot surrender to any enemy, I cannot just weep and die like a helpless widow. I shall fight for my cause and accept death with a smile."

On June 4, the revolution burst in Kanpur. Signs of trouble were seen in Jhansi, the same day. One *havaldar* with a few soldiers entered the Star Fort, which was newly constructed by the British. The soldiers seized the war materials and money from the fort.

There were several instances of mutineers attacking their prisoners, even British women and children. Many atrocities were committed.

Captain Skene and Gordon replaced the more experienced and sympathetic, Ellis and Malcolm. They headed the British force in Jhansi. The British officers requested Rani and asked for her help. To which she clarified that she is neither equipped with an army nor weapons. Instead she suggested getting an army together to protect the people. When the news of the mutiny in Meerut reached Jhansi, she asked permission to raise a small group of bodyguards for her own protection. Captain Skene agreed to this. Skene and the other British officers failed to take Rani's lead to protect them against a possible mutiny. The British who had agreed to Rani's proposal were alarmed when the soldiers shot and killed a British officer the very next day.

Chapter 13

Revolt in Jhansi

On June 5, the members of Jhansi garrison mutinied. They took over two important forts in the town. They killed two of the British officers and wounded another. They plundered town and released the prisoners from the prison.

At once, the senior officer raced to the Rani. He requested Lakshmibai to afford shelter to their women and children at her palace. Her friends advised her to not make any such promises. But she strongly stated that the war is against the Englishmen and not against women and children. If I cannot check our soldiers in this matter, how can I be their leader? The English women and children will get shelter in the palace immediately."

The rest moved to Town Fort. There were 61 people including women and children. The others who sheltered in the town escaped with the help of the local people. The survivors in the Town Fort appealed for Rani's help. So, the Rani not only provided them shelter, but also fed and took care of them throughout the war.

❖ *Know About Rani Lakshmibai* ❖

She had nothing more than a limited military force, small group of bodyguards granted by the British at the onset of the mutiny. She had no obvious political influence over the mutineers. They owed no commitment to the Rani.

On June 7, the mutineers besieged the Town Fort. The mutineers granted safe passage, but just outside Jhansi, in Jokan Bagh, one of the rebel leaders ordered their deaths.

This was described as the Sepoy Mutiny in the accounts written by the British rulers. This gave an impression of sole participation of the soldiers in the revolt. Undoubtedly, the soldiers leaded this people's war, but the Rajas, Maharajas, Chieftains, Peshwas, Nawabs and the Emperors of Delhi, as well as the Hindus, Muslims, *'moulvis'* and *'purohits'* also joined the revolt.

The revolt continued for eighteen to twenty months. Despite of not having a leader, the revolting army scored victory against the British. The soldiers, who had killed the British, demanded three lakh rupees as they had to go to Delhi. They threatened to destroy the palace if the Rani did not agree to pay the money. The Rani then gave her jewels and money to the mutineers, but only under the threat of deposing her in favour of a relative of Gangadhar Rao's, Sadasheo Rao Narain, and, possibly, her own death.

Mr. Thornton, the Deputy Collector of Jhansi, reported that she had given the money as payment for the massacre, which was totally planned by her. The mutineers left for Agra and Delhi to join up with the main body of the rebellion on June 11.

Chapter 14
Rani's Control

The rule of the British had ended in Jhansi. Jhansi restored her peace and happiness. But the city was filled with corpses and the streets were littered with broken guns and war materials. There was chaos in the city. The Rani took immediate action to end the anarchy.

On June 12, Rani wrote a letter to the British, in which she gave an account of what had happened, steps she had

taken to stabilise the situation and asked for help. She wrote a second letter on June 14. She reported the status of Jhansi to the British and again asked for help and orders.

The letters were sent to Major Erskine, who was the Commissioner at Sagar. He forwarded them to Kolkata with a note that the account given "agreed with what I have heard from other sources." On July 2, Major Erskine replied by asking her to manage Jhansi until a new superintendent was sent. Erskine's initiative was not well received by Canning and he sent a letter saying that the Governor-General did not blame him for believing Rani's account, but she would not be protected if her account is proved false. Major Ellis had reported in a telegram that she was forced to help the mutineers with guns, men and money. Despite evidence, the view of her willing assistance seemed to have coloured the perception of the British from thenceforth.

The Rani took Erskine's request seriously and formed a government. Once again, the flag of the state waved gaily on the top of the fort of Jhansi. She took over the reins of administration in Jhansi but the challenges were frightening.

During the regime of Dalhousie, her efficient and loyal officers had been dislocated and migrated to other places. Now, she fell short of far-sighted ministers and veteran generals who could give her sober and practical advice. She was thirty-two years old and solely had to rely on her

own wisdom. The challenges were tough. But her courage and maturity stood the test, and she guided the affairs of the state extremely well. She was also friendly with the British officers, still in Jhansi.

Jhansi was prepared for war. People worked day and night. New arms were manufactured. But amidst such preparations, a new danger confronted Rani.

Enemies of Jhansi were eager to battle and were now prepared to attack the city. The Rani realised the necessity to expand her forces. She freshly recruited soldiers and trained them to fight. One of the rulers in Maharashtra, Sadashiva Rao, laid siege to Kathura, a fort some thirty miles from Jhansi, and seized it. He declared himself as the ruler of Jhansi and directed every village to pay him tribute. He sent messengers to publicise his orders.

When Lakshmibai heard the news, she was infuriated. She expected that the representatives of the British, whom she had befriended, would come to her assistance but they did not turn up. Other chiefs had started to challenge her authority.

Chapter 15
Encounter with Sathe Khan

By then, Rani's forces had strengthened. She pounced on Sadashiva Rao. He was unable to defeat her mightiness and ran away to find refuge in a friend's fort. But after sometime, he dared to attack Jhansi again. The Rani once again swooped down on him and put his army to flight. Rani easily foiled him and took him as her prisoner. But as Jhansi was trying to recover from this danger, in the meantime, Sathe Khan, a minister of the state of Orchha and the Commander of its forces, marched to Jhansi. The forces of Orchha laid siege to Jhansi from October 3 to October 22, while claiming to be acting for the British.

His army consisted of twenty thousand soldiers. Rani suffered heavily and many of her army men were dead or severely wounded or maimed. Rani's advisers and generals recommended that she should consider the possibility of defeat and the consequences. She received an insulting message from the Khan, stating, "If you concede victory and surrender the fort, I shall grant you the pension which the East India Company used to pay."

Know About Rani Lakshmibai

This message immensely enraged her. She summoned her advisers, generals and leading citizens and encouraged them to save the reputation of Jhansi. Inspired by her courageous appeal, they responded bravely. They swore to fight till their last breath for the respect of their motherland. The Rani herself led the army and swooped down on the Khan. His army could not defend against the fury of her attack. She struck like lightning, and, was killing the enemy soldiers by the sword as well as exhorting her soldiers to teach the Khan a lesson. She seemed omnipresent. Sathe Khan ran away from the battlefield.

In order to invigorate her regime, Lakshmibai learnt the art of generalship and improved the army and defences of Jhansi. She also established contact with the rebels, who were the only force who could provide her with the military aid she needed. These events prepared her for her final confrontation with the British. Apart from her expertise in military and administration, due to her late husband's prime interest in theatre, she sifted through the books in the library and encouraged plays at the court.

Such was her valiance that even without an ordered army, she was able to save the city more than once . The people loved and revered her. Her systematic planning and innate courage thrilled the army. And therefore, the army remained dedicated to defend the city with renewed confidence.

Rani Lakshmibai proved to be a competent administrator. She knew that she should keep a vigilant

eye on her ministers, generals and high officials without making it too obvious. She never depended on any individual, no matter how able he proved himself to be.

She still managed to take out time to read the scriptures and the great epics for worship and prayer.

Chapter 16
The Return of the British

By the end of 1857, the British having dealt with bigger problems of Delhi and Avadh, turned their attention to the smaller ones, like Jhansi. The Rani had received no further communications from the British. On 1 January 1858, she wrote to Sir Robert Hamilton to clarify the position of Jhansi. She received no reply to this communication either.

A British force under Sir Hugh Rose, accompanied by Hamilton, marched towards Jhansi on 6 January 1858. Such advancement forewarned her to prepare for the worst.

The approaching force did not intend to just replace the murdered officials but also to execute the mutineers they had captured, and anyone least suspected as a rebel. They also resorted to extensive plundering.

Many including Lord Ginning, the Governor General, and Queen Victoria objected to such crude behaviour. Dr. Thomas Lowe, who was the medical officer with Rose's

force at Jhansi, dismissed such considerations as 'mawkish sentimentality'. Lowe's opinion of Lakshmibai was typical of many British, she was 'the Jezebel of India... the young, energetic, proud, uncompromising Rani, and her head rested the blood of the British slain, a punishment as awful awaited her'.

Within a period of ten months from June 1857 to March 1858, Rani Lakshmibai improved the conditions of Jhansi. The treasury was full. She had raised a force of 14,000 volunteers and 1,500 sepoys, made contact with the rebels, strengthened the defences and prepared for the arrival of the British.

Chapter 17
Rani's Defence

On 7 February 1858, Sir Robert Hamilton sent a report saying, "Although the Rani proposes not to fight against the British government, yet she makes severe hostile arrangements. Six new large guns have been manufactured; carriages for the old and new are in the course of construction. About 200 mounds of saltpetre purchased in the Gwalior district had been bought into the fort. Gunpowder is made within the fort. Eight gunners from

the Moorar rebels were sent from Kalpi and have been taken into service. They superintend the manufacturing of brass balls..."

On 14 February, a proclamation was issued in her name calling on both Hindu and Muslim Rajas to rebel against the British. This marked as a definite sign for revolt if this was issued under her authorisation. However, the British intelligence reports stated otherwise. Her advisors could not take a decision. Even when her father agreed to oppose the British force, she hesitated.

So, irrespective of her feelings, Lakshmibai was at the nexus of a set of forces propelling her to rebel. The British had already thought her to be guilty, and in any case were intent on punishing Jhansi. The townspeople had suffered British rule and were better off under their own rulers. Additionally, the British had failed to respect the Indian customs.

Rani's army, originally raised to defend Jhansi against Orchha, was predominantly composed of rebels and mutineers. They perceived the act of surrendering equal to death. Her father had goals to recover the Jhansi throne for her. She had little choice.

The Rani named some of her guns as '*Mighty Road*', '*Bhavani Shankar*' and '*Lightning Streak*'. Old weapons were sharpened. New weapons were made. During those days, every house in Jhansi was busy preparing for the war under the guidance of the Rani Lakshmibai.

Sir Hugh Rose sent word to the Maharani to come unarmed along with her friends to meet him, but Rani denied. She blatantly refused coming to any place without the protection of her army.

Chapter 18
The Siege of Jhansi

On 21 March 1858, the British forces captured Jhansi. The town was given the option to surrender, but even though Lakshmibai had little choice, she refused. The sepoys whom she had employed were mutineers and therefore had to face execution.

Godse mentioned in the letter that was sent to Rani to urgently meet 'the Captain' with her principal ministers unarmed and unaccompanied. Lakshmibai strictly denied terming it unreasonable and suggested to send the Prime Minister instead, with an armed escort. From the other side, the *Aide de Camp* to General Rose, Lieutenant Lyster mentioned the negotiations between the Rani and Sir Robert Hamilton for surrendering Jhansi and justifying Rose's dissatisfaction with the progress. The British left no record of the negotiations.

The British army, under Sir Hugh Rose, declared war on 23 March 1858. For ten or twelve days, the small state of Jhansi fought with the British. The relief of one success was followed by the shock of another defeat. Many faithful '*Sardars*' died. Unfortunately, Rani received no external help.

14,000 volunteers from a population of 250,000, showed a considerable level of support for Lakshmibai. She also organised women to keep the troops supplied at the frontage.

The British officers observed an enthusiasm and energy in the defending troops that they had never seen in their own native soldiers. Truly, enthusiasm is no substitute for training, discipline, weaponry and leadership in the form of qualified officers. Numerically, the British were greatly outnumbered and their military had the advantage.

Chapter 19
The Battle Continued

For 10 days, the British constantly bombarded Jhansi with artillery. The counter-attack was as intense as the bombardment. Previously, the rebels were able to make a good escape but Rose was determined to not let that happen this time and had surrounded the Fort from all sides.

On March 30, before the British could enter the town, a rebel force of 20,000 under the command of Tantia Tope arrived. Rose divided his forces and defeated the rebel force at the Betwa River. Hundreds of rebels lost, but the British lost less than one hundred.

With the defeat of the rebel force, Rose was able to turn his attention back to Jhansi by April 2. At three o' clock, the next morning, British forces stormed into Jhansi. It was an intense fighting, with the Rani in the thick of it, directing and encouraging her soldiers. At some point, she decided to leave Jhansi.

Despite the precautions taken by Rose, she was able to escape with a small party, including her father. She rode with Damodar tied to her back. How she and her party managed to get through the British lines is still a

mystery. Some say that it was a calculated strategy by Rose, treachery by some of the Indian soldiers employed by the British, negligence by the British soldiers who had left their post to loot, or just sheer courage on the part of Lakshmibai.

Another daring young woman, Jhalkari Korin is believed to have impersonated as the Rani so as to get captured by the British. She was unmasked only when she was brought before Rose. The consequences of which is still unknown.

Chapter 20

Jhalkari Korin

Rani and Jhalkari Korin led the *Durga Dal*, or women's army to constantly foil attacks against the British army. Jhansi fort could not remain invincible for a long time due to the betrayal of one of Rani's generals.

Her appearance, which was strikingly similar to Rani Lakshmibai helped the army to evolve a military strategy to deceive the British. Jhalkari was an ordinary village girl from Bundelkhand who took care of household chores besides tending cattle and collecting firewood from the jungle.

She once encountered a tiger in the jungle and killed the beast with her axe. In another incident, she challenged a gang of dacoits, who raided the house of a village businessman and forced them to retreat.

As a mark of gratitude, the village arranged her marriage with Pooran Kori who matched her in courage. Pooran was inducted into Lakshmibai's army and his fighting skills were soon recognised among her generals.

Once on the occasion of Gauri Puja, Jhalkari with other village women arrived at Jhansi fort to pay homage to the queen.

Rani was struck by Jhalkari's uncanny resemblance to her. She ordered Jhalkari's induction into the *Durga Dal* after hearing such instances of her courage. Jhalkari, along with the other village women, was trained in shooting and igniting the cannons at the time when the army of Jhansi was being strengthened to face any British intrusion.

The British did not allow the childless Rani to adopt her successor, so as to stop her from bringing the state under her control. However, her generals and the people of Jhansi rallied in support of the queen and were determined to fight against the British instead of surrendering to them.

During April 1858, from inside the Jhansi fort, the queen led her army and repulsed several attacks by the British and their native allies. Betraying her, one of her commanders opened a well secured gate of the fort. When the fall of the fortress became imminent, her generals advised Rani to escape with a handful of fighters. The Rani slipped away from Jhansi on the horseback.

Jhalkari's husband, Pooran was killed while he was defending the fort. But instead of mourning her loss, she worked out a plan to deceive the British. She dressed up like Rani and took command of the Jhansi army. Afterwards, she marched out of the fort towards the camp of British General Hugh Rose. After reaching the British enclave, she shouted that she wanted to meet the general.

Rose and his men were exultant. Besides capturing Jhansi, the British thought they had caught the queen alive. When the general, thinking her to be the queen, asked Jhalkari what should be done to her, she firmly said, "Hang me." Such an act of bravery and sacrifice can never be forgotten!

Chapter 21
The Real Jhansi Massacre

The fight continued in Jhansi. The next day also marked continued street fighting, looting, plundering, destruction and murder. A Hindu priest, Vishnu Godse, wrote about his experiences and recalled those four days of fire, pillage, murder and looting without distinction. Rose had instructed his troops to spare none over sixteen except

women. Those who could not escape threw themselves with their wives and children in the wells of the town. As Godse states:

"After the massacre and looting had finished, in the squares of the city,... hundreds of corpses were collected in large heaps and covered with wood, floorboards and anything that came handy, and set on fire. Now every square blazed with burning bodies and the city looked like one vast burning ground... It became difficult to breathe as the air stank with the odour of burning human flesh and the stench of rotting animals in the streets."

Godse's account is in conformity with the British claim that they killed only the men, the deaths of women was more or less accidental in general. He reports four days of unsystematic massacre of men and systematic looting.

The original mutineers of Jhansi, the 12th Bengal Native Infantry, who were in Lahore, were all killed while defending the fort.

Rani's had two encounters while escaping. The most famous is that of Lieutenant Dowker, who by his own account pursued her until he got shot by the Rani herself thus disabling him. According to other Indian sources, he was wounded in a sword fight with the Rani at a village called Bhander.

The second account, from Cornet Combe was set in the village of Banda: "We sent all over the country in pursuit of the Rani and one of our troops overtook her at a place called Banda, 20 miles off. Her escort made a hard fight of it, and though our fellows did their utmost and killed every man, she got away, her smart saddle falling into our hands."

She covered 100 miles to Kalpi in a day. She was given a procession of honour on her arrival.

Her father, among others, was not so fortunate. He was wounded, while he was leaving Jhansi, and somehow managed to reach Datia. But on reaching, he was handed to the British and was hanged in Jokhan Bagh.

Chapter 22
The Final Battle

A rebel force under Tantia Tope went to Koonch, where Rose, after a delay of three weeks, went on to defeat them on May 6. Thereafter, Rose advanced to Kalpi. There, the rebels were demoralised, but were inspired by the arrival of the Nawab of Banda, and the nephew of Nana Sahib, Rao Sahib. Encouraged by the reinforcements

and Lakshmibai's promise to fight with them till the end, they attacked the British on May 22.

Despite being considerably weakened by the scorching heat of the midday sun, the British were able to defeat the rebels, who were forced to draw back. This time they went to Godalpur, outside Gwalior where instead of surrendering, they daringly decided to take on Gwalior. The fort at Gwalior was architecturally strong and virtually impregnable. The ruler, Maharaja Scindhia, had maintained a pro-British stance throughout the rebellion.

The rebels advanced to Gwalior with 11,000 men, where they met Maharaja Scindhia at Morar. After the first shots were fired, the rebels defeated the Maharaja, and the Maharaja left to Agra for safety. Rao Sahib was

crowned at Gwalior and Lakshmibai was gifted a priceless pearl necklace from the Gwalior treasury.

Rose advanced his force towards Gwalior. Lakshmibai was given command of the eastern border, the most difficult to defend, and met the British at Kotah ki-Serai on June 17. She 'dressed as a man' but with bangles and the pearl necklace. Her troops loved her. The place, time and manner of her death is not certain. There are several accounts. According to some sources, she was killed on the parapets of Gwalior. According to others, she was killed at Kotah-ki-Serai.

Two days later, the rebels left Gwalior, not attempting to hold what was known as a virtually impregnable position. The death of Lakshmibai absolutely demoralised them. The British easily retook the fort of Gwalior. The rebellion was over.

Chapter 23
Account of Rani's Death

The most credible account was given by Lord Canning in his papers: "Rani of Jhansi, killed by a trooper of the 8th Hussars, who was never discovered. Shot in the back, her horse drew back. She then fired at the man, and he passed his sword through her. She used to dress like a man, wore a turban and rode like one... not pretty, and pockmarked with smallpox, but was elegant and had beautiful eyes. She wore gold anklets, and Scindhia's pearl necklace, plundered from Gwalior. She distributed these among the soldiers when taken to die under the mango clump... The infantry attacked cavalry for allowing her to be killed. The cavalry said that she rode too far in front. Her tent was very coquettish.... Two maids of honour rode with her. One was killed, and in her agony the other stripped off her clothes. The army mourned the Rani for two days."

Another similar version by J. Henry Sylvester, says, "The gallant Queen of Jhansi fell from a carbine wound, and was carried to the rear, where she expired, and was burnt according to the custom of the Hindus." An excerpt

❖ Know About Rani Lakshmibai ❖

from the diary of Edward Gret, a veterinary surgeon, 8th Hussars, gives his account "The Rani was on horseback... when the British cavalry, 8th Hussars, made their surprise appearance, causing her escort to scatter... she boldly 'attacked one of the 8th in their advance, was unhorsed and wounded', possibly by a saber cut. A short while later as the British retired, she recognised her former assailant as she sat bleeding by the roadside and fired at him with her pistol. Unfortunately she missed and he 'dispatched the young lady with his carbine'. But because she was 'dressed as a sowar', the trooper never realised that he had cut off one of the mainstays of the mutiny, that there was a reward on his victim's head, or the fact that she was wearing jewels worth a crore of rupees."

Understandably, the Rani's funeral was carried out very quickly after her death, since none could guarantee whether she would be respectfully cremated if delayed. In Sir Hugh Rose's report, he mentions her funeral and affirms that she was buried 'with great ceremony under a tamarind tree under the Rock of Gwalior'.

Lakshmibai had two 'maids of honour' who accompanied her from Jhansi namely, Mandar and Kashi Kumbin. Mandar is a childhood friend of Lakshmibai and was killed in the same incident in which Lakshmibai was fatally wounded, while Kashi had to stay back to look after Damodar. It was Kashi, according to Devi, who prepared Rani for her funeral pyre, and who with another close attendant of Rani, looked after Damodar for two years before surrendering him to the British after guaranteeing his safety. They are revered for their loyalty and courage.

Chapter 24

A Glorious Woman

Rani Lakshmibai of Jhansi emanated glory and reverence. Her life was a holy bliss, a thrilling story of striving excellence, courage, adventure, selfless patriotism and martyrdom.

She embodied the spirit of a lioness in her tender body. She was well versed and proficient in statesmanship.

She went to war and faced every consequence with utter bravery. She reflected the image of Kali, the goddess of war. She was young in years, but was foresighted and ensued maturity in her decisions.

She was an ideal daughter and an ideal wife. Even after the death of her husband, she did not let go of her responsibilities. She was a staunch Hindu, but was tolerant of other religions, and therefore could lead a great army.

Lakshmibai lived for 29 years and seven months, from 19 November 1828 to 18 June 1858. She sparkled and vanished like a lightning on a dark night.

Even the British General, Sir Hugh Rose, who fought against Rani swore on her greatness: "Of the mutineers, the bravest and the greatest commander was the Rani."

www.ingramcontent.com/pod-product-compliance
Lightning Source LLC
LaVergne TN
LVHW091317080426
835510LV00007B/527